IN THE SHADOW OF THE ANGELS

JAMES RUDY GRAY

In the Shadow of the Angels

Copyright © 2021 James Rudy Gray
AA, BA, MA, ThM, DMin

All Rights Reserved.

Scripture taken from the New American Standard Bible,
Copyright 1960, 1962, 1963, 1972, 1973, 1975, 1977, 1995 by
The Lockman Foundation. Used by permission. wwwLockman.org.

Cover painting of the Charleston Angel Oak
By Katy Neely, Katyneelyart.com

ISBN 978-1-940645-97-1

Greenville, South Carolina

Published in the United States of America

Dedication

To our "angel" grandchildren: Gray, Ben, Sylas, and Eli —
and to God's angels who watch over His people

Table of Contents

Foreword vii

Introduction xi

Chapter 1: Angels Are Real 17

Chapter 2: Angels Are Watching Over Us 27

Chapter 3: Angels Are Soldiers 37

Chapter 4: Jesus and Angels 45

Chapter 5: The Angel of the Lord 55

Chapter 6: When Humans Are Angels 63

Chapter 7: Fallen Angels 73

Conclusion 81

Resources 85

Charleston Angel Oak
By Katy Neely
Katyneelyart.com

Foreword

If you ask ten people on the street what they believe about angels, you will probably get ten different answers. If you ask ten church members what they believe about angels, don't be surprised to hear ten different answers from this group as well. Based on some of the things I have heard as a pastor for nearly forty years, it seems like many church members' understanding of angels has been influenced as much by fiction (e.g., *It's A Wonderful Life*) as by Scripture.

Test your knowledge of angels: Are all angels uniquely created by God, or do some people become angels after death? Does the word "angel" mean "messenger," or does "angel" mean "spirit/ghost"? Should human beings worship angels, or are they servants of God who are never to be worshiped? Do Christians ever encounter angels today, or did encounters with angels cease when the Bible was completed?

The answers to these and other questions about angels will be answered in the following pages of Dr. Rudy Gray's latest book, *In the Shadow of the Angels*. For almost forty years, I have known Rudy as a Christian brother, fellow pastor, wise counselor, and trusted friend. But in more recent years, I have also come to know him as a helpful writer. Rudy's book, *Marriage That Works Is Work*, has become my textbook for premarital counseling. This new book on angels will become my number one recommended resource for anyone looking for answers to questions about angels.

As you would expect from a pastor-theologian like Dr. Gray, he provides a biblically sound overview of the subject of angels. He does a great job of correcting some of the common misconceptions about angels by providing clear, straightforward, biblical teaching. When it comes to what might be called "gray matters," he points out relevant Scripture, provides opinions of respected Christian authors, but wisely leaves questions the Bible does not answer unanswered.

You would also expect a veteran pastor and counselor like Rudy to share stories from people who have encountered angels. He not only does that, but also shares how an angel intervened in his own life-threatening experience. Some of you may think, "Here's where it's going to get weird." But you are wrong. The stories that Rudy shares about Christians who have had personal encounters with angels are supernatural, but not sensational. I know some of the individuals named in this book who describe their encounter with an angel, and can testify that they are level-headed, biblically grounded Christians. They are simply sharing their experiences of being chosen by God to receive His gracious blessing of encouragement, comfort, protection, or rescue through the ministry of an angel.

I am confident that Dr. Gray's *In the Shadow of the Angels* will provide you with a valuable biblical and practical resource for gaining a better understanding of God's special messengers. In addition, the story of "The White Minivan" in chapter 6 will motivate you to become a more active "human angel" in ministry to others. It is my prayer that God will use this book to increase your knowledge of the Bible's teaching about angels, and to increase your awareness of how God continues to use angels in our lives today.

Fred Stone, Pastor
First Baptist Church
Pickens, South Carolina

Introduction

As believers, we live in the shadow of the angels. "Shadow" is a fascinating word, and most of us know its normal or typical meaning. However, when shadow is used as a verb, it means to follow someone closely or secretly. It has the idea of a dominant presence or influence and conveys the thought of being nearby or in a close vicinity.

Angels shadow us. They follow us. Psalm 23:6 says, "Surely (or only) goodness and mercy will follow me all the days of my life." The ancient theologians referred to goodness and mercy as the hounds of heaven. Goodness supplies our needs, and mercy (or lovingkindness) blots out our sins.

What an amazing truth! God's goodness and mercy follow us wherever we go, and I believe that angels are often used by God to bring that goodness and mercy into our lives.

Before the creation of the earth or mankind, angels existed. They have always gone about their great ministry unnoticed. Angels were created by God for His own glory and to serve Him through serving His people. They are eternal and immortal. They look at the lives of humans and marvel at God's redemption of lost people. They cannot be saved because they have not sinned, but they do rejoice in heaven when someone is born again.

The angels watch us, follow us, and get involved in this world as directed by God — and that's when it gets interesting! Throughout human history, stories of mysterious visitors, miraculous interventions, and unimagined results abound. Behind it all stands a great, sovereign God with His enormous army of angels who are ready to obey His every directive. In this book, I share several stories of angelic involvement in the lives of people.

Angels are great, but they refuse to be worshiped, and we are warned in Scripture not to worship them. They are spirit beings and invisible to the human eye. Yet, on some rare occasions they have appeared in the form of a human being. When people have encountered an angel or angels, they were almost always unaware of it at the time. With complete unanimity, those who have had an encounter with one of heaven's angels did not seek it.

We meet them in the pages of the Bible, worshiping and praising God in heaven and serving God's people on earth through guidance, protection, encouragement, deliverance and much more. Angels are literally messengers who bring us a message from God.

Angels are not on the minds of most people, and I am convinced that is just fine with them. The world has a tendency to exalt them to a position of worship, which leads to heresy or an outright denial of their existence and contributes to spiritual deafness.

It is my hope and prayer that as you read this book, you will be moved to praise God for His eternal, invisible, and incredible angels. We walk in the shadow of these majestic and powerful spirits of God.

IN THE SHADOW OF THE ANGELS

Chapter 1

ANGELS ARE REAL

Angels are real. They appear in the pages of Scripture and in the lives of believers throughout the ages. Unlike fictional superheroes or mythical characters, they move back and forth between the dimension of heaven and the dimension of earth. They are almost always invisible, but they are always incredible and amazing. Although most of us will never see an angel, on rare occasions they appear in human form. I have never seen an angel, but I believe an angel appearing in human form did intervene in my life in the fall of 1997.

I was part of a mission team that year that spent several days in a remote mountain region of Honduras. For multiple reasons, I slept very little during the seven days we were serving the Honduran people. All of us were tired when the time came for us to return to our homes in the States.

We left Honduras early that morning for New Orleans, where we were scheduled to catch a connecting flight to

Atlanta. When we landed in New Orleans, my friend Wayne Dickard received a phone call informing him that one of his brothers had died. It was a sad time, and many of us gathered around him to pray. Soon, we prepared to exit New Orleans.

Exhausted and sleep-deprived for over a week, I boarded the plane. Wayne sat beside me and offered to share the newspaper he was reading with me. I told him I just wanted to rest. Shortly after the plane was airborne, I fell asleep. Sometime later, I was awakened by Wayne, who was kneeling over me in the aisle of the plane. He said, "You need to be still. Something bad has happened." I was confused and had no idea what had occurred. Two medical doctors were leaning over me. We were given emergency status to land in Atlanta, and I was taken to a local hospital. Medical personnel immediately began a battery of tests. They first thought I had a brain tumor, but later, based on blood tests, determined I had suffered a heart attack with likely damage to the heart muscle. As a pastor, I had spent many hours in hospitals visiting with church members and others, but this was my first experience as a hospital patient.

During the time of testing, probing and prodding, I sensed an unusual peace, and, despite all the serious implications of my condition, I was able to relax. I heard a distinct nonverbal message reverberating in my soul, "You are going to be okay." I did not interpret that to mean that I would be okay physically, but that I was going be okay whether I lived or died.

I had spoken with my wife, Anne, by phone before going to the hospital, assuring her that I would be home soon. At that time, she was an algebra teacher and administrator in a Christian school and was having some back problems, which limited her activities. We first decided that she did not need to come to Atlanta. Later, Teresa Keese, the director of the school and a close personal friend, drove Anne to the hospital in Atlanta.

When they arrived, the medical tests had already been completed, including a nuclear stress test. We waited for the results. The cardiologist came by my room and told me he was going to discharge me. I was excited and did not ask any questions. My wife had missed the doctor but wanted some of her questions answered. She was told that they "could not find anything wrong" with my heart. There was no damage to the heart muscle. We left the hospital and drove back to South Carolina.

About two weeks later, Wayne and pastor Wilson Nelson, who were on the mission trip with me, asked me to meet them for lunch in a nearby town because they had something to share with me. Since I was unconscious during the trauma on the plane, I had no recall of what had happened. They told me that a woman wearing blue jeans, a brown leather jacket, and a baseball cap stood over my shoulder while the doctors helped me. Some people thought I had died because I was not breathing. Just before they attempted a tracheotomy, the doctors turned me on my side. I started to breathe. To this day, Wayne says, "I am telling you that you died on that plane!"

The woman with the blue jeans, brown leather jacket, and baseball cap did not talk to anyone on our mission team, and none of them knew who she was. While she was standing over my shoulder, several people from our mission team formed prayer circles in the aisle of the plane and called out to God to help me. Wilson, with tears rolling down his cheeks, asked God to save my life and raise me up. He said, "I am not sure how long that went on or how it was received by the other passengers on the flight, but I know all of your fellow pilgrims on this flight were calling out to Jesus for you. There were many audible, loud prayers being lifted up on your behalf with great emotion."

Can you imagine that scene: Christians agonizing in prayer on a plane more than 31,000 feet in the air — many concerned that I had passed away. Most of the passengers on the plane were not part of our mission team, and undoubtedly some of them were not Christians. Can you picture their shocked reaction when this man who appeared to be dead walked off the airplane? I was quickly placed in a wheelchair in the terminal area. I was not planning on going to the hospital at that time — but in the terminal, Joan Penn, a member of the mission team and a nurse from our church, noticed I had my hand on my chest and immediately asked if I was hurting. I denied I was in pain, but it was too late. She summoned her husband and they drove me to the hospital.

Another of Wayne's brothers, Robert, and his wife, Faye — along with Wayne's wife, Anita — drove to the Atlanta airport to pick up Wayne. Robert parked in the Delta terminal area while the two women went inside to get Wayne. Robert stayed in the van. Very soon, a woman wearing blue jeans, a baseball cap, and a brown leather jacket exited the terminal and walked directly to his van. She approached the driver's side and said, "You are waiting for the mission team from Honduras to return, aren't you?" He replied in the affirmative, and she responded, "Pastor Gray has had a seizure on the plane and is being taken to the hospital, but he is going to be okay. His wife, Anne, is coming to Atlanta to be with him. If you will watch my bag, I will bring your wife to you." Just a couple of minutes later, this mysterious woman came back to the van with Faye in tow. This angelic messenger held them both by the hand and said again that I was going to be okay.

When Wayne and Wilson told me this story, I immediately remembered the message I received in my heart at the hospital: "You are going to be okay." This woman had delivered the exact same message. She could not have known Anne was coming to Atlanta because that decision had not even been made at that point. She knew Anne's name and details about our lives that, to this day, still baffle us.

Was this person one of God's angels? I think so. I believe God sent an angel into my life, although I never saw her.

The late Billy Graham said that he had sensed the presence of angels in his life on special occasions. Popular pastor Tony Evans has stressed that if we learn to see the unseen, we will see more than we ever imagined. In her song, "This Is My Story," the remarkable blind poet and hymn writer Fanny Crosby stated, "Angels descending, bring from above, echoes of mercy, whispers of love." Mary Anne Evans, writing under the pen name George Eliot, wrote, "The golden moments in the stream of life rush past us and we see nothing but sand; the angels come to visit us, and we only know them when they are gone." Francis of de Sales said, "Make yourself familiar with the angels, and behold them frequently in spirit; for, without being seen, they are present with you." James Russell, American poet and diplomat, said, "All God's angels come to us disguised."

The word "angel" occurs approximately 287 times in the Bible. That number can change according to the English translation a person uses. Hebrews 12:22 refers to myriads of angels. A myriad is 10,000. "Myriads" means literally tens of thousands. The phrase suggests a number beyond our comprehension.

Angels are spirit beings. There are other types of spirit beings mentioned in the Bible, such as seraphim, cherubim, and the living creatures of Ezekiel and Revelation. There are also other types of spiritual beings other than God's elect (or good) angels. These fallen angels (or demons), along with their leader, Satan, will be the focus of a later chapter.

Angels can touch people if necessary. When Herod had Peter arrested and imprisoned, an angel came to his rescue. Acts 12:7 says, "An angel of the Lord suddenly appeared, and a light shone in the cell; and he struck Peter's side and roused him, saying, 'Get up quickly.' And his chains fell off his hands." It is interesting in the verses that follow this account that the angel would not do for Peter what Peter could do for himself. After the angel led him out of the prison, verse 11 says that when Peter came to himself, he said, "Now I know for sure that the Lord has sent forth His angel and rescued me from the hand of Herod and from all that the Jewish people were expecting."

John Calvin wrote, "Scripture teaches that believers have the constant presence of the Holy Spirit (Ephesians 3:16, etc.), that the Holy Spirit sometimes guides by external means, and that occasionally angels are released from heaven for particular tasks" (Acts 8:26). Calvin did not believe that every believer has a special guardian angel, but that "our care is not the task of one angel only, but all, with one consent, watch over our salvation." Theologian Wayne Grudem agreed, stating, "The angels may be playing 'zone' rather than 'man-on-man' defense."

Hebrews 1:5-2:9 clearly teaches that Christ is superior to angels, and Colossians 2:18 and Revelation 22:8-9 indicate that Christ alone is to be worshiped. Angels should be respected and appreciated but not worshiped. We believe in Christ for salvation and trust what the Bible teaches about angels — God's special created order of servants who serve Him by serving those who are born again. Calvin notes, "The angels are the dispensers and administrators of the divine beneficence toward us; they regard our safety, undertake our defense, direct our ways, and exercise a constant solicitude that no evil befall us."

Angels rank lower than Jesus and higher than humans. They are powerful, intelligent, and seek to always honor and serve God. They are amazed at God's salvation of people and look with intense interest at God's miraculous work of redemption (1 Peter 1:12). Jesus said in Luke 15:10 that there is "joy in the presence of the angels of God over one sinner who repents." They are deeply interested in taking care of God's children and are always available to come to our aid, even though God does not always allow them to do so (Hebrews 1:14).

They love God supremely, follow Him with steadfast loyalty, and obey Him absolutely. Angels never come between believers and God. They serve believers because of their great love for God. They can influence our minds and hearts for good. It appears they not only have a tremendous interest in spiritual things, but also in the physical and material well-being of God's children. Theologian Charles Hodge wrote, "What they are able to accomplish in the material or external world is greater than our comprehension."

Early Southern Baptist leader James Petigru Boyce

observed that angels "have a deep interest in people and become the medium of messages to them." There are many stories of mysterious people helping God's servants at critical times in their lives. These compelling accounts point to the presence of an angel. For example, a seminary professor shared the story of a missionary he knew who had an encounter with an angel. The missionary was looking for answers, struggling with his life and ministry. As he drove to a preaching assignment, he prayed for God to give him guidance. The rain was heavy as he noticed a man hitchhiking in the storm. The missionary stopped and offered the man a ride. As the two traveled on together, the missionary discovered that this hitchhiker was a strong and knowledgeable Christian who offered him some great insights. They stopped at a diner for coffee and continued to talk. After bidding each other goodbye, they parted ways. As the missionary drove away, he realized he had not even gotten the hitchhiker's name. He turned around and headed back to the diner and asked the waitress which direction the man who was with him had gone. She replied, "What man? I wondered why you ordered two cups of coffee." He returned to his car, realizing that the stranger had not seemed wet, even though he was walking in a drenching storm.

    John Woolmer, in his book, *Angels*, wrote, "Whenever men and women encounter supernatural beings, there is a measure of confusion. Angels often do look like human beings. Only subsequently, often after a mysterious appearance, do people realize the full significance of what has happened."

Angels are real, and they are all around us. We may never see an angelic appearance, but we can be certain of their powerful and benevolent presence.

Chapter 2

ANGELS ARE WATCHING OVER US

All night, all day
Angels watching over me, my Lord.
All night, all day,
Angels watching over me.

The song "Angels Watching Over Me" may date back to the days of slavery and was possibly composed by an African-American in the Deep South. Otis Leon McCoy — who was born in Ninety-Six, South Carolina, in 1897 — is credited as the writer or arranger of the song, but may not have been the original author. The message behind the song is both simple and powerful: Angels are watching over us.

God's angels do watch over His children. They are present in our lives, even when we do not realize it. Sandy Smith was a mother with two small daughters in Clemson, South Carolina. One evening she had a strong need to visit with her parents in nearby Easley.

"As I was driving to their home, I sensed a compelling need to pray for my dad's relationship with Jesus, which I did," she said. When she got to the house, she found him reading a Bible she had never seen before. It turned out that he had inadvertently picked up the Bible along with his personal papers at the store of a customer. Sandy said, "As I sat down beside Dad, I was immediately aware of a spiritual presence in the area behind his chair. I heard and felt air movement, like the wind. Looking in that direction, I saw nothing. That night was a turning point in my dad's life. When I left that evening, I knew there had been an unseen presence in the room. It was not until years later that I put it all together. Watching God work with my dad during the ensuing six years, until his death at sixty-five, was a beautiful picture of God's grace in action. My dad died content with life and at peace with God."

Angels rarely appear to us in this world. Most often, we sense a presence similar to what Sandy experienced — something different, special, unusual, and even mysterious.

Angels appeared to people in the Bible, and have appeared to people since the Bible was completed. However, from all the evidence, no one who had an encounter with an angel sought it. In fact, they typically did not know they had been visited by an angel until the angel was gone.

Whether angels appear or not, they are constantly watching over believers. They observe our lives: our obedience and disobedience to God, our struggles and temptations, our needs and wants, our gratitude or ingratitude, and all the ups and downs we experience.

In the Old Testament, the story of Daniel in the den of lions is inspiring and illustrative of God's care for His people through the agency of angels. Daniel was one of the three cabinet members in King Darius' court, but the other two — along with many others in positions of power — did not like Daniel. They persuaded Darius to sign into law an injunction that could not be changed (the law of the Medes and Persians). It was simple but deadly: No one was allowed to pray to any god or man except the king — and if they did, they were to be thrown into the den of lions. Daniel 6:10 says, "Now when Daniel knew that the document was signed, he entered his house (now in his roof chamber he had windows open toward Jerusalem); and he continued kneeling on his knees three times a day, praying and giving thanks before his God, as he had been doing previously." Daniel's enemies found him violating the law and brought the evidence before the king. Darius was troubled and contemplated releasing Daniel, but the law had to be followed.

Just before he threw Daniel into the den of lions (think capital punishment), Darius said, "Your God whom you constantly serve will Himself deliver you" (v. 16). Daniel was thrown into the den of lions, and the entrance was sealed with a large stone. That night the king could not sleep. Early the next morning, he ran to the den of lions and called to Daniel in great distress, "Daniel, servant of the living God, has your God, whom you constantly serve, been able to deliver you from the lions?" (v. 20).

Maybe there was a moment of silence just before Daniel said, "My God sent His angel and shut the lions' mouths, and they have not harmed me" (v. 22). An angel was watching over Daniel and protecting him. Darius ordered the instigators of this unjust law to be sentenced to the den of lions. Daniel 6:24 says, "They cast them, their children, and their wives into the lions' den; and they had not reached the bottom of the den before the lions overpowered them and crushed all their bones." Darius then made a decree that all the people in his kingdom were "to fear and tremble before the God of Daniel, for He is the living God and enduring forever" (v. 26).

Following a great movement of God in Jerusalem, the high priest and his supporters were overcome with jealousy and had the apostles thrown in jail. Acts 5:19-20 records what happened next. "But an angel of the Lord during the night opened the gates of the prison, and taking them out he said, 'Go your way, stand and speak to the people in the temple the whole message of this life.'" The guards could not find them and were perplexed. They found them in the temple teaching the people. An angel watched over them and freed them from prison.

A massive earthquake hit Haiti in 2010. A group of Christians from Greenville, South Carolina — including medical personnel and other volunteers — went to the island to help. Mark and Sarah Lynch were part of that group. Mark said, "We saw a lot of death and miracles. Twenty-one days after the earthquake hit, a man was found under large pieces of concrete. The Haitian workers had already started bulldozing dead bodies. It took a lot of work to get him out, but he was alive. We could hardly believe it. We had to work hard at keeping ourselves hydrated daily, and he had been under this pile of rubble for twenty-one days."

How did he survive? Two natives who spoke Creole interpreted what the rescued man shared. "He said a man in a long white robe came to him every day and gave him water. He was very grateful," Mark said.

Who was the stranger in a white robe that gave the man water daily? Apparently, no one but the rescued man knew about this stranger. He certainly could have been an angel.

Landrum Leavell, late president of New Orleans Baptist Theological Seminary, believed that angels primarily minister to us on this earth in physical ways. He observed, "I believe they (angels) are available to us in the fulfillment of our prayers in the will of God every minute of every day."

Pastor Ron Fousek and his wife, Jewel, received a blessing and a miracle from God. The news was delivered by angels. After fourteen years of marriage, the couple was unable to conceive — although they had prayed fervently for a child. Ron says their prayers were simply, "God, give us a child." The church he pastored was praying the same prayer. They underwent treatments for infertility. He says, "We were confident that everything was really going to lead to our becoming a mom and dad."

In the fall of 1977, Ron shared that Dr. Robert Greenblatt, a highly respected endocrinologist, "told us that we would not be able to have a child." The surgeon recommended a hysterectomy for Jewel in January 1978. Ron says, "This time we prayed, 'Lord, whatever You want of us, even it is not Your will for us to have a child, we will accept it.'" Both he and Jewel said they had "a peace that passed all understanding" about this decision.

Ron says, "About this time, in the middle of the night, I was peacefully awakened with no unsettled feelings at all. I sat up in bed and noticed some movement over in the corner of the room. Still, I had nothing but a settled peace. There they stood — two tall, white-robed beings talking with each other and pointing in the direction of me and my wife as if to pass a message to us. They caught my attention, and, with a pleasant expression and nod, they were gone. Amazingly, I went back to sleep. It was not yet the time for me to digest what this visit by two angels meant for us."

What happened next is Ron's story of how angels watch over us.

"Jewel was admitted to the University Hospital in Augusta, Georgia, for her surgery on Monday. Early Monday morning, Jewel went in for surgery, while her parents, a friend, and I waited. Shortly after the surgery was to begin (too soon), I received word that the doctor wanted to see me. I was alarmed. As I made my way down the hallway, Dr. Greenblatt's assistant came to me, saying, 'Your wife is pregnant! Your wife is pregnant!' As I stood there stunned, Dr. Greenblatt said the same thing and grabbed me with a big bear hug. He explained that they put Jewel to sleep and made the incision. Then, just before he started the procedure, he noticed, to his surprise, that Jewel was pregnant — around seven weeks. He stopped everything, closed the incision, and gave her an injection to help with the development of the baby's lungs. Later when I told Jewel that she had not had surgery, but was going to have a baby, she was speechless, but responded with happy tears streaming down her cheeks." As he thought about the timeline, he recalled that her pregnancy of seven weeks corresponded to the night the two angels visited them.

In August of 1978, their son was born with what Ron says was excellent health. "When we stopped praying selfishly and yielded to what God wanted for us, the miracle was set in place. The angels were sent forth to make the announcement. These emissaries from heaven carried the message from the throne of God, and we are forever grateful to Him." Today, his son is married and has two children. Ron and Jewel have a grandson and a granddaughter. God delivered the miracle. Angels brought the message.

Charles Spurgeon wrote, "If mysterious temptations

come to you, there shall also be mysterious defenders to thrust them back. If all men forsake you, God can send His angels, though you see them not, to strengthen you in some secret manner that I cannot fully explain."

Angels often are the carrier of messages that confirm, support, encourage, warn, or simply help us. In his book, *Angels: God's Secret Agents,* Billy Graham wrote about an unusual story he got from *Reader's Digest.* Neurologist S.W. Mitchell was awakened late one night by a knocking at his door. When he opened the door, a young girl told him her mother was very sick and needed a doctor. Dr. Mitchell followed the girl into the cold, snowy night. When they arrived at the little girl's home, he discovered her mother was seriously ill with pneumonia. He sent for additional medical help and complimented the mother on the determination of her daughter. Somewhat shocked, the mother replied, "My daughter died a month ago. Her shoes and coat are in the closet there." Bewildered, the doctor opened the closet door and saw what looked like the same coat the little girl was wearing, but it was dry and warm — which would have been impossible after walking through the snow and cold. Graham concluded, "Could the doctor have been called in the hour of desperate need by an angel who appeared as this woman's young daughter?"

Don Bradley grew up in Illinois with an alcoholic father who physically abused his mother. His dad lost job after job and even stole money from his son to buy alcohol. Don attended church with his mother until she stopped going because of the bruising on her arms from her husband's abuse. At thirteen, Don made a profession of faith and was baptized. He eventually became a successful businessman and served as a deacon at Utica Baptist Church in Seneca, South Carolina. His mother died from complications of Alzheimer's disease at age ninety. He says, "I know I am going to heaven by the grace of God, because I grew up on the wrong side of the tracks and nobody would ever think I would be a Christian."

A few years after his mother died, he found himself involved in church but not as committed as he felt he should be. One Sunday morning as he walked to the stage to lead in the morning prayer, he saw a woman sitting on the end of the front pew dressed like his mother used to dress. He was stunned by what was happening. She nodded at him and smiled as if to encourage him. "I will never forget that," he says. "It touched me forever. Just as suddenly as she appeared, she was gone." From that day on, he began to read and study his Bible daily, attend every church service, pray daily, and get involved with community Bible study. He's eighty-six now and says he has a wonderful peace. That Sunday morning in church, he believes an angel appeared as his mother with a simple, yet powerful, message of encouragement.

Angels cannot, and do not, attempt to replace God. Angels have been referred to as God's ministry staff. They serve God and obey Him as He leads them to serve others. When angels have appeared, the people to whom they appeared never expected, sought, or asked for angel help.

Chapter 3

ANGELS ARE SOLDIERS

Angels are soldiers in God's spiritual special forces. The word "soldier" simply means "one who serves in an army or an active follower." As a verb, it means "to carry on or move onward with persistence, determination, and perseverance." A soldier is a person under orders. Good soldiers are obedient, loyal, faithful, and skilled as warriors. Soldiers have different ranks from private to general. Angels have ranks as well. For example, Michael is referred to as an archangel and Gabriel is recognized as a high-ranking angel, although Scripture does not say he is an archangel. His name means "God's mighty one."

The seraphim are part of the special angelic order, with an emphasis on preserving and protecting God's holiness around the throne as they praise and adore Him. The cherubim are mentioned in Genesis 3:24, and seraphim are named in Isaiah. The hymn "Holy, Holy, Holy" by John Bacchus Dykes and Reginald Heber seems to capture the essence of these two types of spirit beings in the second stanza: "Cherubim and seraphim falling down before Thee, who was, and is, and evermore shall be."

God's angel army carries out His will in various and sundry ways. Angel soldiers protect, defend, rescue, and provide whatever assistance and intervention God decrees. They are engaged in an ongoing war with demonic spirits (fallen angels) in the spiritual realm. A case in point is Daniel 10, where the prophet had received a vision that exhausted him and caused him to fall into a deep sleep. When he awoke, a hand touched him, and he was shaken. In verses 12 and 13, this visitor said to Daniel, "Do not be afraid, Daniel, for from the first day that you set your heart on understanding this and on humbling yourself before your God, your words were heard, and I have come in response to your words. But the prince of the kingdom of Persia was withstanding me for twenty-one days; then behold, Michael, one of the chief princes, came to help me, for I had been left there with the kings of Persia."

Many believe this angel who came to Daniel was Gabriel, who is mentioned in Daniel 8:16 and 9:21. The demon assigned to Persia by Satan was able to prevent this angel from getting his message to Daniel. During the twenty-one-day delay as a great spiritual battle was being fought between the forces of good and evil, Daniel prayed and fasted.

It has been observed that prayer is absolutely essential

in the life of a Christian — and in this passage from Daniel, we are given a brief picture into the spirit world, where spiritual warfare continually rages between Satan and his forces against God and His angel soldiers. It is alarming that our prayer lives can be so disrupted and neglected. There is a powerful demonic system that works to keep us from praying and deceives us into praying with little faith and even less persistence. In Romans 15:30, Paul wrote, "Now I urge you, brethren, by our Lord Jesus Christ and by the love of the Spirit, to strive together with me in your prayers to God for me." The same apostle wrote in Ephesians 6:12 that "our struggle is not against flesh and blood, but against the rulers, against the powers, against the world forces of this darkness, against the spiritual forces of wickedness in the heavenly places." After instructing believers to put on the full armor of God, he wrote in verse 18, "With all prayer and petition pray at all times in the Spirit, and with this in view, be on the alert with all perseverance and petition for all the saints." Jesus gave us a model to follow, or pattern to use, when we pray (Matthew 6:9-13). First Thessalonians 5:17 counsels us to "pray without ceasing."

Colossians 4:2 tells us to "devote yourselves to prayer, keeping alert in it with an attitude of thanksgiving." Jesus gave a parable in Luke 18 regarding a persistent widow and an unjust judge. Luke 18:1 says, "Now He was telling them a parable to show that at all times they ought to pray and not to lose heart." The judge finally relented and gave the widow the justice she requested. In contrast, God will quickly provide answers to our prayers if we pray with persistence. Don't give up praying. Angels themselves are often involved in bringing God's answers to our prayers.

The devil and his troops work to keep us from prayer, but, like God's angel soldiers, we must be persistent — praying when we feel like it, and when we don't.

The angel brought Daniel a message of hope for the future of God's people. That passage reveals that the angel fought against the demon assigned to Persia not to destroy Persia, but to influence the king to show favor to God's people in Persia.

There is a widely circulated story from World War I regarding angel soldiers. Several eyewitnesses have shared details of the amazing narrative. The British soldiers were retreating through Belgium with the German military charging after them in what, by all indications, would be a great victory for the Germans. Suddenly, the Germans began to open fire on a vacant field. The British watched in amazement as the German army pounded the empty field with artillery and machine-gun fire — enough to eliminate anyone in the area. German soldiers who were captured following the battle reported that there was a large body of mounted soldiers clad in white uniforms riding horses. They stated, "We saw the shells breaking into death-dealing fragments and bursting amidst their ranks with shattering crashes, which shook the ground. But the White Cavalry came quietly forward at a slow trot, and not a man or a horse fell. They advanced with their leader, a fine figure of a man. By his side was a great sword and his hands lay quietly holding the reins of his great white charger."

Terror seized the Germans, and they began to flee, throwing down their weapons and running away from something they could not understand and could not stop. One soldier emphasized that even though the fighting might continue, Germany lost the war that day, beaten by the mysterious and invincible white cavalry. Were the stories of the German soldiers true or merely hallucinations? Were these impressive beings angel soldiers?

Corrie ten Boom, the heroic Christian who protected many Jews during World War II before her own internment in a German concentration camp, also experienced God's angel army.

After the war, she was serving in a school for missionary children in the Congo. Approximately 200 missionary children were being taught there. The leaders of the mission heard that hundreds of rebel soldiers were coming to kill everyone in the mission. One night the rebels came, but as they drew closer to the compound, suddenly they stopped and fled. That was repeated for three consecutive nights.

Later, one of the rebels who had been wounded was brought to the mission compound for treatment. While the doctor was treating him, he asked the man why they did not attack the school. The rebel reported that they could not because, "We saw hundreds of soldiers in white uniforms and became scared." Did the rebels encounter God's angel soldiers?

In nearly every book about angels, the story of John Paton, missionary to the New Hebrides, is shared. Paton told about a particular night when wild cannibals began to dance in a frenzy around the Patons' house. The people inside did not know what to expect, but they prepared for the worst. They cried out to God in prayer. Shortly after they started to pray, the intruders returned to the jungle. A year later, the chief of that tribe became a Christian, and Paton asked him why he and his men did not attack the house that night. The man replied, "Because of those men you had with you." The chief said they saw hundreds of big men in shining clothes with swords in their hands circling his home. Did God send His angel soldiers to protect the missionary family?

Psalm 34:7 says, "The angel of the Lord encamps around those who fear Him and rescues them." The phrase "angel of the Lord" most frequently means the incarnate Christ, but sometimes it means an angel representing the Lord. What many commentators and Bible students see in this verse is a group of angels, guided by a lead angel — maybe Christ incarnate. The imagery is staggering: God's people completely surrounded by angel soldiers.

An ancient writer described a Turkish encampment near Cairo where the bashaw's palatial tent was surrounded by 200 tents, laid out in such a way that the opening of each tent's doors looked out toward their leader's tent. The layout was designed to protect the royals occupying the dwelling in the center.

Calvin wrote that the doctrine of Scripture teaches that the angels encamp around the godly (Psalm 34:7), meaning not simply one angel, but many. This picture is like that of a contingent of soldiers surrounding people for their protection, defense, and rescue.

There is something like a parallel dimension that exists all around us. In that space, angels and demons move. We almost never see them, but on some rare occasions we may get a glimpse of this unseen reality. When Jesus was transfigured with Moses and Elijah in Matthew 17, Peter was absolutely amazed at what he was seeing. He was ready to build tents for them and stay on the mountain. When Jesus was ascending into heaven following His resurrection, we get a glimpse into that dimension. Acts 1:9-11 is simply awesome: "And after He had said these things, He was lifted up while they were looking on, and a cloud received Him out of their sight. And as they were gazing intently into the sky while He was departing, behold, two men in white clothing stood beside them; and they also said, 'Men of Galilee, why do you stand looking into the sky? This Jesus, who has been taken up from you into heaven, will come in just the same way as you have watched Him go into heaven." The two men were certainly angels, but the bigger question is where did they come from? How did Jesus go into the presence of the Father? It was not like He flew out of earth's atmosphere to another planet. He simply went up in the air and stepped into the other dimension — not one where angels and demons battle, but where God sits upon His throne.

Just before Stephen was stoned to death for preaching the gospel, Acts 7:55 says, "But being full of the Holy Spirit, he gazed intently into heaven and saw the glory of God, and Jesus standing at the right hand of God." Stephen did not see a distant place, but he was given the privilege to see into the other dimension just before he died.

Angels and demons are constantly engaged in spiritual warfare in the dimension around us. We do not see it, but it is happening. Believers often face danger and opportunity, unaware that evil stalks them while God's angels protect them.

Chapter 4

JESUS AND ANGELS

During Jesus' earthly life, angels were a significant part of His work. The angel Gabriel was sent by God with a message for Zacharias, a priest in Israel, and his wife, Elizabeth. The couple had no children, and Luke says they were "advanced in years." The angel of the Lord appeared to Zacharias while he was performing his duties in the temple. When he saw Gabriel, he was anxious, prompting the angel to comfort him. The message was nothing short of spectacular — Zacharias and Elizabeth were going to have a baby boy! Gabriel encouraged Zacharias, and told him his son would preach in the spirit and power of Elijah and would be a forerunner for the coming Messiah, preparing the people for Jesus' coming.

Zacharias questioned the seeming impossibility of him and his wife having a child. The angel replied to him, "I am Gabriel, who stands in the presence of God; and I have been sent to speak to you, and to bring you this good news" (Luke 1:19).

A short time later, Gabriel was sent to a virgin in Nazareth named Mary. He gave Mary the most astonishing news in history — she was chosen to be the mother of Jesus. Her conception would not come in the natural way, but from God — and the child she would give birth to would be called the Son of God. Gabriel reminded her that "nothing will be impossible with God" (Luke 1:37).

Mary's response was exemplary when she answered Gabriel: "Behold, the bondslave of the Lord; be it done to me according to your word" (Luke 1:38). Luke then says simply that "the angel departed from her."

Angels do not compete with Jesus, but rather they worship, serve, praise, adore, obey and glorify Him. From before His birth to His death, resurrection and second coming, angels serve the King of kings and Lord of lords.

John was born to Zacharias and Elizabeth — and, soon after, Jesus was born to Joseph and Mary in Bethlehem. In fact, when Jesus was born, shepherds were tending their flocks just outside of Bethlehem when "an angel of the Lord suddenly stood before them, and the glory of the Lord shone around them; and they were terribly frightened" (Luke 2:9). The heavenly messenger comforted them and counseled them not to be afraid but to go to Bethlehem — where they would find the newborn Messiah wrapped in cloths, lying in a manger. Luke 2:13-15 says, "Suddenly there appeared with the angel a multitude of the heavenly host praising

God, and saying, 'Glory to God in the highest, and on earth peace among men with whom He is well pleased.' And it came about when the angels had gone away from them into heaven, the shepherds began saying to one another, 'Let us go straight to Bethlehem then, and see this thing that has happened which the Lord has made known to us.'"

Sometime later, Magi from the east came to worship Jesus. Trouble was brewing as King Herod was insanely jealous and insecure. He felt threatened that a Jewish baby had been born in his jurisdiction and was being called the king of the Jews by mysterious visitors from the east. His idea was to find the location of the Messiah child and destroy him. The Magi, after presenting their expensive gifts to Joseph and Mary, returned to their homeland, bypassing Herod and Jerusalem. When the Magi left, "an angel of the Lord appeared to Joseph in a dream" (Matthew 2:13), advising him to take his family away because Herod was planning to destroy Jesus. The young family left for Egypt, as Herod had all the boys killed in and around Bethlehem who were two years old or younger.

A few years later, Herod died. Matthew 2:19-20 says, "But when Herod was dead, behold, an angel of the Lord appeared in a dream to Joseph in Egypt, saying, 'Arise and take the Child and His mother, and go into the land of Israel; for those who sought the Child's life are dead.'"

Back in Jerusalem, Jesus grew in grace, knowledge, and wisdom. When it was time for Him to begin His ministry on earth, He approached John the Baptist, Zacharias and Elizabeth's son, who was serving God as the forerunner for the Messiah. Jesus presented Himself to John for baptism in the Jordan River. At Jesus' request, John baptized Jesus. After this, Jesus was led by the Spirit into the wilderness, where He fasted for forty days and nights. He was hungry and physically exhausted. At that time of bodily weakness, the devil tempted the Savior with three of the greatest temptations ever faced by a human being. After Jesus defeated Satan by quoting Scripture with each temptation, the devil retreated. Matthew 4:11 says, "Then the devil left Him; and behold, angels came and began to minister to Him."

Throughout Jesus' ministry on earth, angels were always around Him — unseen guardians ready to serve and protect Him as God allowed. When Jesus was in His early thirties, the time for Him to sacrifice His life for our sin came. It was orchestrated through the evil and hateful actions of the religious leaders of the day — but, make no mistake, it was decreed by God. Jesus' mission on earth was not just to teach the highest and greatest truths, but to be the sacrifice for the sin of all people. Jesus knew His mission, and even though He was the most unique person in history — all God, and all man — He felt the weight of His burden.

In a garden called Gethsemane, Jesus went to pray with His disciples. The pressure on Him was supernaturally intense. In His agony, His sweat became like drops of blood. Luke 22:43 says, "Now an angel from heaven appeared to Him, strengthening Him." While in the garden, Judas Iscariot led the evil and unjust Jewish leaders, with Roman officials, to arrest Jesus. Peter wanted none of that and pulled his sword, amputating the ear of the high priest's slave. Jesus calmly healed the slave's ear and said to Peter, "Put your sword back into its place; for all those who take up the sword shall perish by the sword. Or do you think that I cannot appeal to My Father, and He will at once put at My disposal more than twelve legions of angels?" (Matthew 26:52-53). The common number of a legion was 6,000, so twelve legions would be 72,000 angels. Don't you know they were ready, willing and able to destroy their Lord's enemies? But it was not God's will.

Following His Gethsemane arrest, Jesus went through the mockery of a trial and was sentenced to be executed on trumped-up charges. He was beaten, mocked, ridiculed, and nailed to a cross to die like a guilty criminal. Through His horrific crucifixion, He remained committed to the will of the Father. He knew that His mission was to seek and to save the lost.

When He died, they took His body from the cross and buried Him in a borrowed tomb. The Jewish leaders thought that was the end of the story, but it was only the beginning. Matthew 28:2-3 says, "A severe earthquake had occurred, for an angel of the Lord descended from heaven and came and rolled away the stone and sat upon it. And his appearance was like lightning, and his garment as white as snow."

The Roman guards were gripped with fear and froze like dead men. The women who had come to His grave encountered a powerful surprise. Matthew 28:5-6 says an angel said to the women, "Do not be afraid; for I know that you are looking for Jesus who has been crucified. He is not here, for He has risen, just as He said." Mark says the women entered the tomb and saw a young man dressed in a white robe. Luke wrote that two men in dazzling apparel stood near the women. John wrote that Mary "was standing outside the tomb weeping; and so, as she wept, she stooped and looked into the tomb; and she saw two angels in white sitting, one at the head and one at the feet, where the body of Jesus had been lying" (John 20:11-12).

Woolmer wrote about the four differing accounts of the angels at the tomb and explained why he believes they are slightly different. "Whenever men and women encounter supernatural beings, there is a measure of confusion. Angels often do look like human beings. Only subsequently, often after a mysterious appearance, do people realize the full significance of what has happened. The discrepancies in the accounts of the first Easter Day render the narrative more, not less, authentic."

Following His resurrection, Jesus appeared to more than 500 witnesses during the forty days before His ascension. In the sight of many witnesses in Acts 1, Jesus ascended back to the Father in heaven. Two angels stood with the group.

Angels were around Jesus throughout His life on earth and with Him when He entered into the presence of His Father in heaven.

One day in the future, angels will be with Jesus when He comes again. In Matthew 24, Jesus warned His followers that false Christs and false prophets would come, but one day He would send out His angels "with a great trumpet and they will gather together His elect from the four winds, from one end of the sky to the other" (Matthew 24:31).

First Thessalonians 4:16-17 says, "For the Lord Himself will descend from heaven with a shout, with the voice of the archangel, and with the trumpet of God; and the dead in Christ shall rise first. Then we who are alive and remain shall be caught up together with them in the clouds to meet the Lord in the air, and thus we shall always be with the Lord."

From the beginning of history until its end, angels are involved. They will be involved in the return of Jesus to earth and will continue to serve in the new heaven and the new earth.

Life on this earth is brief — and the older we grow, the more we realize the inevitability of death. What happens at death? For Christians, we leave this body and enter into the presence of God forever. But what about the moment of death? Landrum Leavell wrote, "I believe when a child of God dies, in the moment, in the split second that life ceases in his body, the spirit made in the image of God rejoins God. That spirit will be escorted into the presence of Almighty God by our personal angel and possibly others."

Jesus taught in John 14 that in His Father's house are many dwelling places (rooms, abodes, mansions) and that He has prepared a place for us. Many Bible students believe that when a believer dies, he or she is escorted into God's presence by the angels. David Jeremiah stated, "Why dread that moment of death? The journey to heaven will not be dark, fearful, or lonesome. God will dispatch His angels at just the right time, and they will meet us just within the veil and carry us to the heights of His glory."

In Luke 16, Jesus told the story of a godless rich man and a godly poor man named Lazarus. The rich man died and lifted up his eyes in Hades. But for Lazarus, it was very different. Luke 16:22 says, "Now it came about that the poor man died and he was carried away by the angels to Abraham's bosom … ." Notice that Lazarus was carried into the presence of God by angels.

Jeremiah believes angels will escort us into the presence of God. "Death may sound fearsome, but not when we're looking to Jesus. There's no denying Christians have a different way of dying than non-Christians. I can assure you angels are real. They are God's real estate agents, ready to show us our heavenly homes and move us into mansions

Jesus has prepared for us."

Various artists and singers have tried to assure believers with their music that God's angels will be with us in the time of death. The old song "Angel Band," written in the mid 1800s, captured that idea in the words, "Oh, come angel band, come and around me, stand. Oh, bear me away on your snow-white wings to my immortal home."

The old spiritual "Swing Low, Sweet Chariot" also captures the same hope: "I looked over Jordan and what did I see, coming for to carry me home! A band of angels coming after me, coming for to carry me home." When Charles Haddon Spurgeon was on his deathbed, the man who has been called the greatest preacher in the English language said, "I can hear them coming! Don't you hear them? This is my coronation day. I can see chariots. I'm ready to board." He died on January 31, 1892, at the age of fifty-seven — no doubt escorted by angels into the presence of Jesus.

Billy Graham wrote, "The Scripture says there is a time to be born and a time to die. And when my time to die comes, an angel will be there to comfort me. He will give me peace and joy even at that most critical hour, and usher me into the presence of God, and I will dwell with the Lord forever. Thank God for the ministry of His blessed angels."

Jesus has always been around angels. These special messengers of God have served Him faithfully for thousands of years. They will never lead us to worship anything but

God, and they will never allow people to worship them. They are God's servants. When Jesus returns, angels will be with Him — and whether we meet Christ in the air or meet Him through the transition of death, angels will be there.

Chapter 5

THE ANGEL OF THE LORD

The angel of the Lord is mentioned several times in the Old Testament and none in the New Testament. Why? The angel of the Lord, on just about every occasion, is an appearance of God in a visible form — an incarnation. The International Standard Bible Encyclopedia makes an interesting observation regarding the angel of the Lord: "It is obvious that these apparitions cannot be the Almighty Himself, whom no man has seen or can see. He is 1) an angel with a special commission, 2) a momentary descent of God into visibility, or 3) a temporary preincarnation of the second person of the Trinity."

Some writers call the angel of the Lord the "angel of the theophany," or the "angel who carries God's presence." Overwhelmingly, the phrase is referring to God Himself, with some references indicating a high-ranking angel who is speaking for God.

When there is some type of visible appearance of God

in the Old Testament, we can be confident it is the Son of God. He is the only person of the Trinity to be incarnated into human flesh. The Trinity — Father, Son, and Holy Spirit — have always existed. The oneness of God is revealed in three distinct but inseparable persons. The Angel of the Lord is not mentioned in the New Testament, except when an Old Testament reference is used, because God incarnate had come to live on earth. Jesus Christ was the most amazing person in human history — fully God and fully man. He was the "God man." Someone once observed that Jesus was older than His mother and as old as His Father! To claim to be God is blasphemy, unless it is true. Jesus said in John 8:58, "Truly, truly I say to you, before Abraham was born, I am." Jesus is also referred to as the Word. John 1:1 says, "In the beginning was the Word, and the Word was with God, and the Word was God." Verse 14 says, "And the Word became flesh, and dwelt among us, and we beheld His glory, glory as of the only begotten from the Father, full of grace and truth."

There is no theophany in the New Testament because God was with us in the flesh through the incarnation of Christ. One of the giants in Southern Baptist life, W.A. Criswell, used to say that the only God we would ever see is Jesus because Jesus was God incarnate.

When we think of the Angel of the Lord, we are not really talking about an angel (in nearly all instances) but God Himself. In Genesis 16, the story of Hagar — Sarai's maid and mother of Abram's son Ishmael — is recorded. Hagar was treated badly by Sarai, even though Sarai had suggested that Abram father children with her since Sarai seemed unable to conceive. Sarai changed her mind and treated Hagar harshly. Hagar fled to the wilderness, where the angel of the Lord found her. He told her to return to Sarai and promised He would greatly multiply her descendants to such a degree that they would be too many to count. Genesis 16:11 says the Angel of the Lord came to her, saying, "Behold, you are with child, and you shall bear a son; and you shall call his name Ishmael, because the Lord has given heed to your affliction." Verse 13 says, "Then she called the name of the Lord who spoke to her, 'Thou art a God who sees'; for she said, 'Have I even remained alive here after seeing Him?'"

In Genesis 18, three men visited Abraham — two angels and the Angel of the Lord. Abraham was told by the Angel of the Lord that Sarah (by this time her name had changed from Sarai to Sarah, and his name from Abram to Abraham) would conceive and bear a son. The men began their journey to Sodom. Abraham tried to negotiate with the Angel of the Lord by asking Him to spare Sodom if He found fifty, forty-five, forty, thirty, twenty, and, finally, ten righteous people there. The Angel of the Lord said in verse 32 that He would not destroy the wicked and perverted city if there were only ten found. Verse 33 says, "And as soon as He had finished speaking to Abraham, the Lord departed ... ." The two angels proceeded to Sodom.

In Genesis 22, the Angel of the Lord stopped Abraham from sacrificing his son Isaac. As he was about to kill his son with a knife, verse 11 says, "The angel of the Lord called to him from heaven and said, 'Abraham, Abraham!' And he said, 'Here I am.'" Later, the Angel of the Lord blessed Abraham for his willingness to obey the Lord even if it meant sacrificing his son and said, "In your seed all the nations of the earth shall be blessed, because you have obeyed My voice" (v. 18).

In Genesis 32, Jacob is on his way to try and make peace with his estranged brother, Esau. He crossed the Jabbok stream after leaving his family and children behind. Genesis 32:24-30 gives an amazing account of the Angel of the Lord engaging a human being:

> Then Jacob was left alone, and a man wrestled with him until daybreak. And when he saw that he had not prevailed against him, he touched the socket of his thigh, so the socket of Jacob's thigh was dislocated while he wrestled with him. Then he said, "Let me go, for the dawn is breaking." But he said, "I will not let you go unless you bless me." So he said to him, "What is your name?" And he said, "Jacob." And he said, "Your name shall no longer be Jacob, but Israel; for you have striven with God and with men and have prevailed." Then Jacob asked him and said, "Please

tell me your name." But he said, "Why is it that you ask my name?" And he blessed him there. So Jacob named the place Peniel, for he said, "I have seen God face to face, yet my life has been preserved."

While Moses was tending his sheep, the Angel of the Lord appeared to him. Exodus 3:2 says, "And the angel of the Lord appeared to him in a blazing fire from the midst of a bush; and he looked, and behold, the bush was burning with fire, yet the bush was not consumed." Moses was instructed to remove his sandals as the Angel of Lord identified Himself (v. 6): "I am the God of your father, the God of Abraham, the God of Isaac, and the God of Jacob." Moses then hid his face "for he was afraid to look at God."

In Joshua 5, the Angel of the Lord is identified as the captain of the host of the Lord. He appeared to Joshua before the miracle at Jericho. Joshua asked in verse 14, "What has my lord to say to his servant?" Verse 15 says, "The captain of the lord's host said to Joshua, 'Remove your sandals from your feet, for the place where you are standing is holy.' And Joshua did so." Joshua obeyed the Lord, even though the orders sounded strange. The result was that the so-called impregnable walls of Jericho fell down.

In Judges 6, Gideon encountered the Angel of the Lord. Verse 12 says the Angel of the Lord appeared to him. Verse 14 says that "the Lord looked at him," and in verse 16 "the Lord said to him." After assuring Gideon He would be with him, the Angel of the Lord received a sacrifice from him. Verse 22 says, "When Gideon saw that he was the angel of the Lord, he said, 'Alas, O Lord God! For now I have seen the angel of the Lord face to face.'" Verse 23 says, "And the Lord said to him, 'Peace to you, do not fear, you shall not die.'" The Angel of the Lord in this passage is also referred to as the Lord because it is the preincarnate God who appears, the second person of the Trinity.

Hezekiah prayed for God to deliver his people from the wicked and powerful king of Assyria. The Assyrians had destroyed people and their idols as they conquered groups and nations. Judah was at risk. God promised Hezekiah that the king of Assyria would not come to the city or even shoot an arrow, but that God Himself would defend the city for His own sake and the sake of His faithful servant David. Second Kings 19:35-37 says, "Then it happened that night that the angel of the Lord went out, and struck 185,000 in the camp of the Assyrians; and when men rose early in the morning, behold, all of them were dead. So Sennacherib king of Assyria departed and returned home, and lived at Nineveh." Soon afterward, Sennacherib was killed.

There is at least one example where the angel of the Lord appears, but it is not God. In 2 Samuel 24, King David, in anger, made the decision to conduct a census among the Israelites. The Lord did not command it, but David did it anyway. After his act of disobedience, David's heart was troubled. He confessed to God that he had sinned greatly and asked God to take away his iniquity. The Lord sent a pestilence upon Israel where 70,000 men died. Second Samuel 24:16-17 says, "When the angel stretched his hand toward Jerusalem to destroy it, the Lord relented from the calamity, and said to the angel who destroyed the people, 'It is enough! Now relax your hand!' And the angel of the Lord was by the threshing floor of Araunah the Jebusite. Then David spoke to the Lord when he saw the angel who was striking down the people, and said, 'Behold, it is I who have sinned, and it is I who have done wrong; but these sheep, what have they done? Please let Thy hand be against me and against my father's house.'"

David offered burnt offerings to the Lord and then built an altar to the Lord. God was moved by his sincerity and held back the plague (2 Samuel 24:25).

Isaiah 9:6 says that "a child will be born to us, a son will be given to us." Jesus was incarnated by being born through the virgin Mary. The Child was born, but the Son is given to us. He has always been, and will always be, the Son of God. Louis Goldberg was raised an Orthodox Jew but became a Christian. Still, he had a great heart for the Jewish people and continued to study and research them throughout his life. He was a professor and a pastor, and he observed that "the functions of the Lord in the Old Testament prefigure the reconciling ministry of Jesus. In the New Testament, there is no mention of the angel of the Lord; the Messiah Himself is this person."

It has been said that the Old Testament is the New Testament concealed, and the New Testament is the Old Testament revealed. Jesus in the Old Testament is the Angel of the Lord. Jesus in the New Testament is the Messiah. He died for sin and was raised from the dead. One day He will return and rule this earth, where He at one time walked, taught and lived. Someday there will be a new heaven and a new earth, but Jesus will always be the Son of God: the Angel of the Lord in the Old Testament; the Messiah in the New Testament; and the soon-to-come King of kings and Lord of lords.

In whatever age we examine, Jesus is now, and always will be, God.

Chapter 6

WHEN HUMANS ARE ANGELS

Christians do not become angels when they die. An angel does not get his wings by doing a certain number of good deeds. Angels are spirits and were created by God. However, there is a way that people can be angels — not spirits, but messengers on a mission for God to His people.

The Greek word *angelos* is typically translated "angel" in the Bible, but the word also means "messenger." When applied to people, the *angelos* is a human messenger. Messengers were often sent out on an assignment or mission from God through the church. In Luke 9:52, Jesus sent messengers ahead of Him and His disciples to make arrangements for Him. When God's people follow Christ in obedience, we are also going forth as messengers (*angelos*).

Some Bible students believe Hebrews 13:2 could be referring to human messengers instead of angel spirits: "Do not neglect to show hospitality to strangers, for by this some have entertained angels without knowing it." The idea behind this interpretation is that when Christian servants were sent out to serve and preach, they often faced financial difficulties — perhaps not even having a place to sleep at night. Christians who housed and fed these traveling missionaries, preachers and teachers were actually entertaining God's messengers (*angelos*).

The late F.F. Bruce, a highly regarded British theologian, commented on Hebrews 13:2 by pointing out that the writer of Hebrews "is not necessarily encouraging his readers to expect that those whom they entertain will turn out to be supernatural beings traveling incognito; he is assuring them that some of their visitors will prove to be true messengers of God to them, bringing a greater blessing than they receive."

The point of Hebrews 13:2 is showing hospitality to strangers. Hospitality was practiced in the Middle East during biblical times, and it became a tradition in the early church. We may never see an angel in the sense of a created spirit of God, but we may help a messenger of God by showing hospitality. It is a duty and an opportunity for Christians even today. Some may turn away from this practice, saying there is too much risk involved. We should be careful, but as one preacher put it, "I would rather err on the side of mercy when it comes to helping someone in need." That person in need may be a human angel (messenger).

We often use the word "angel" to apply to a person who

is a blessing. Parents may refer to their children as angels. The use of angel in the context of a human messenger is certainly different than the majority of cases in the Bible where angel spirits are meant.

James 2:25 speaks of Christians demonstrating their faith through works. "Was not Rahab the harlot also justified by works, when she received the messengers (*angelos*) and sent them out by another way?" These messengers were the spies from Israel sent out to scout the land. Mark 1:2, Luke 7:27, Matthew 11:10, and Malachi 3:1 are quoted by Jesus: "Behold, I send My messenger before your face." The messenger in this case was John the Baptist.

Angels are unseen spirit beings. People are not invisible spirit beings, but they can be God's servant messengers. While I was writing this book, I received something written by Emerson Shipe, retired professor and researcher at Clemson University. His account of something very personal to him at a tender time in his life illustrates when humans are angels in the sense of messengers serving God through helping others. We can, in essence, be "earth angels."

The White Minivan
By Emerson Shipe

The early-afternoon midsummer sun was bearing down intensely on the Eugene Shipe farm and his modest home on Bud McMillan Road in Knoxville, Tennessee. My dad had lived, worked the soil, and tended livestock on this piece of God's property for all of his ninety years. My mom, two sisters, and myself were gathered with our families, awaiting my dad's funeral service later that afternoon.

As the family sat quietly in the non-air-conditioned living room in their best Sunday suits and dresses, perspiration was already appearing on our foreheads and darkening the armpits of the men's white shirts. It was a hot and humid July day in East Tennessee. It was the type of day that brought memories of "putting up hay" in nearby fields, sweating, and drinking ice-cold water from the gallon jug that Dad always took to the field for the workday. I sat on the couch with Mother, looking through the front window — somehow both anticipating but yet dreading what was to come.

Only three days earlier, Dad lay still, breathing heavily, in the raised hospital bed in front of that same window. His dying process had been a three-month ordeal. Following congestive heart failure in late April, shortly after his ninetieth birthday celebration, his fragile health had slowly deteriorated day by agonizing day. He was hospitalized for a few days but returned home, asking that he not be taken back where they had stuck and probed him, keeping him awake at night to determine how well he was resting.

My sisters provided loving care and support for Mom and Dad during these months. I was there for a week after he came home from the hospital. He could not lie flat in the bed because of the smothering fluid around his heart and lungs — so he slept in short intervals through the night, partially propped up in a reclining chair. Mother had us move the recliner into their bedroom so she could sleep in their bed but still be near him. He ate little, telling us that he "just wasn't hungry." His weight dropped steadily, leaving his face sunken and his once-strong hands thin and weak. He was so weak he couldn't lift his hand high enough to comb his hair.

In his last few days, we moved him into a hospital bed in the living room. As he slept more and talked even less than before, we observed the purplish-blue discoloration on his feet and ankles move slowly up toward his knees, his heart weakening more and more. He passed away about 5 a.m. on July 23, 1997. He just quit breathing — and I thanked God for a quiet passing of the man who was my best friend and co-cheerleader, along with my mother, for all of my endeavors and accomplishments. He was my greatest teacher.

Two days later as we sat there on the couch, awaiting the half-mile drive down to Union Baptist Church for Dad's funeral, family members were exhausted and anxious. Mother had worn-out arthritic knees, so she used a walker and sometimes a wheelchair if the walking distance was substantial. She was physically and mentally tired. Many encouraging words had been spoken and earnest prayers offered for our family, but we were silently and individually preparing ourselves for a long, emotionally draining afternoon.

As I stared out the front window at nothing in particular, a white minivan appeared and moved slowly up Bud McMillan Road past our house, as if the occupants were searching for a particular address. Thinking it might be extended, and seldom-seen, family members who had come early for the funeral, I walked into the front yard and raised my arm to signal them. The van moved a few yards past the house, turned into a neighbor's driveway, backed out, and then drove back. As I continued to wonder who this might be, the van turned into Mom and Dad's driveway and cautiously approached the house.

There were five occupants in this angel van. They didn't have wings or white robes and did not carry harps. They were dressed, as we were, in funeral attire. As they disembarked, they actually appeared to be friends from the South Carolina church where Pam and I were members. Our pastor, his wife, the music minister and his wife, and one of the deacons from the church slowly emerged from the van as if arriving from a long journey. When they declined to have lunch, which we had recently finished, it was another convincing indication to me that they were angels. I don't think angels need Baptist-prepared ham and fried chicken.

A tear still comes as I remember how their presence just lifted my heart and spirit that day. God sent our angel friends to comfort, encourage, and be present with me and my family during a very sad and stressful time. I don't remember what they said to us, but their presence was all that was needed and more than sufficient. It was as if God's messengers were silently saying, "We are here to come under the heavy burden you carry today." They were more than willing to join in sharing, and even lifting, that load of sorrow and responsibility.

Non-believers will say, "Okay, no big deal. So you had some friends who came to be present at your father's funeral." Even believers might say, "Okay, five Christian friends took time away from their daily duties and work assignments to drive a round trip of 400 miles to encourage Emerson and Pam Shipe's family at his father's funeral."

Others can make their own judgment, but, in my mind and for always, on July 27, 1997, five angels showed up on Bud McMillan Road in a white minivan to minister to me and my family.

The white minivan in that story belonged to me. My wife and three others from our church made the trip from South Carolina to Tennessee that day. I can assure you that none of us are angels from heaven. However, we were messengers on a mission of love and service for some of God's dear servants.

In this sense, any Christian can be an "angel" by simply serving God and others. In fact, we are all called to be God's servants or messengers, even though most of us will never see a visible appearance of an angel from heaven.

We could say that when Christians serve God and others, they are a type of "earth angel" — a born-again person with an eternal soul. An angel of heaven is a created eternal spirit who may, on rare occasions, take the form of a human being.

In Chapters 2 and 3 of Revelation, the leaders (pastors) of the seven churches are called angels. While it is possible that each church was assigned an angel, most scholars and Bible teachers seem to agree that the angels in these two chapters refers to human beings instead of spirit beings. The late pastor J. Vernon McGee took the position that "the angels (to the churches in Revelation 2 and 3) were human messengers serving as teachers and leaders in the churches."

Christians can be used by God as messengers to others. In the larger picture, we could say true Christians and angels are both involved in serving God as messengers, even though heaven's angels work at a superior level with greater strength and intelligence.

Believe in angels, for they are real. Trust fellow Christians who bring us God's message. Serve God, who is the same yesterday, today, and forever. Join with the angels in heaven, who seek to glorify His name.

Chapter 7

FALLEN ANGELS

I wanted to focus on God's good angels only in this book, but I found it increasingly necessary to devote the final chapter to the bad or fallen angels, generally referred to as demons or evil spirits.

Satan (or the devil) was created by God, along with all the other angels. He was known as Lucifer, son of the morning — a light bearer. Some, like W.A. Criswell, J. Vernon McGee, David Jeremiah, and John MacArthur believe his fall is recorded in Ezekiel 28 and Isaiah 14, and that one-third of all the angels created by God fell with him.

Donald Grey Barnhouse wrote, "There came a time when this being, filled with pride because of his own power and attainments, entertained the thought in his heart that he could govern independently of God. He therefore proclaimed that he would set up an independent rule whereupon a multitude of the angelic beings of heaven decided to follow his rule and join him in his rebellion against God."

Following his rebellion, Satan was expelled from heaven, along with an army of fallen angels who he organized into an evil organization with varying ranks and responsibilities. Fallen angels are demons — and since they were created by God, they are much more powerful and intelligent than human beings. However, Christians do not need to be afraid. Through the Holy Spirit, we can overcome the malignant schemes and attacks of Satan and his fallen angels. Our focus must not be on Satan or demons, but on Christ and His power and grace. Remember, spiritual warfare is not God versus Satan as though they were equal combatants. God created Satan! Perhaps that is one reason R.C. Sproul used to say, "The devil is God's devil." Satan can only do what God allows him to do.

In Luke 10, seventy disciples went out on a mission authorized by Jesus. They were amazed at what happened. They said, "Lord, even the demons are subject to us in Your name" (v. 17). Jesus responded to them in verse 18: "I was watching Satan fall from heaven like lightning." He explained to His disciples that He had given them authority over Satan in their mission, but they should not rejoice that the evil spirits were subject to them, but to "rejoice that your names are recorded in heaven" (v. 20).

God's people cannot engage the forces of evil and expect to win because of our intelligence, power, or even strategy. Our human authority is no match for Satan's forces. We must only go into spiritual battles with the authority of Christ Jesus, armed with His Word in our hearts and minds. For guidance, we have the Spirit of Truth, the best GPS possible for navigating the turbulent seas encountered in this present age.

In Ephesians 2:2, the apostle Paul says that unsaved or lost people live "according to the prince of the power of the air, of the spirit that is now working in the sons of disobedience." He goes on to say we all lived in that condition before the new birth. Satan is called the "prince of the power of the air." Those few words have generated a multitude of ideas about what that statement means. It seems to be that dimension around us where demons do their work. The late Ray Stedman wrote that this "may be a metaphorical reference to the fact that as the air pervades our environment and yet is invisible to us, the devil and his (fallen) angels are arrayed against God, surrounding us on every side, invisible, and yet constantly manipulating our minds." In John 12:31, Satan is referred to by Jesus as the "ruler of this world." It is important to always put things into the right perspective. Satan is a powerful evil prince, but Jesus is the omnipotent King of kings and Lord of lords.

Paul wrote in 2 Corinthians 4:3-4, "Even if our gospel is veiled, it is veiled to those who are perishing, in whose case the god of this world has blinded the minds of the unbelieving, that they might not see the light of the gospel of the glory of Christ, who is the image of God." The god of this world (or age) is Satan, but he is not *the* God. Satan is the god of the present age and works mightily through those who live in disobedience to the revelation of the one true God.

How can the followers of Jesus Christ live in an age where Satan dominates? Evil has always infiltrated the earth since the fall. The devil and his army of demons fight against the people of God. First John 3:7-8 says, "Little children, let no one deceive you; the one who practices righteousness is righteous, just as He is righteous; the one who practices sin is of the devil; for the devil has sinned from the beginning. The Son of God appeared for this purpose, that He might destroy the works of the devil." Jesus came to destroy the works of the devil — and even though Satan is allowed to do battle, he is a defeated foe. His fate was sealed forever when Jesus died on the cross. He is active, powerful, and destructive today, but he has already lost the war.

Job said that man is full of trouble as the sparks fly upward. Jesus said in this world we will be pressured. "In the world you have tribulation, but take courage; I have overcome the world" (John 16:33). Paul wrote about spiritual warfare and ended his letter by encouraging believers to "be strong in the Lord, and in the strength of His might" (Ephesians 6:10). He called on believers to put on the full armor of God and described what it was in Ephesians 6:14-18: "Stand firm therefore, having girded your loins with truth, and having put on the breastplate of righteousness, and having shod your feet with the preparation of the gospel of peace; in addition to all, taking up the shield of faith with which you will be able to extinguish all the flaming arrows of the evil one. And take the helmet of salvation, and the sword of the Spirit, which is the Word of God. With all prayer and petition pray at all times in the Spirit, and with this in view, be on the alert with all perseverance and petition for all the saints."

Satan and his army may be defeated, wounded, and headed for eternal torment, but he is active in this age. While recognizing the reality and power of the devil, Peter offers believers some awesome encouragement in 1 Peter 5:8-10: "Be of sober spirit, be on the alert. Your adversary, the devil, prowls about like a roaring lion, seeking someone to devour. But resist him, firm in your faith, knowing that the same experiences of suffering are being accomplished by your brethren who are in the world. And after you have suffered for a little while, the God of all grace, who called you to His eternal glory in Christ, will Himself perfect, confirm, strengthen and establish you."

Satan wants to destroy us, but God wants to bless us and use us to glorify His name. Don't forget that Satan was originally an angel created by God. He is a fallen angel, but God is greater than His creation — which includes both good and fallen angels, as well as the devil himself. No better comparison between Satan and God's Son can be found than the one in John 10:10: "The thief comes only to steal, and kill, and destroy; I came that they may have life, and have it abundantly." The devil is a liar and the father of lies. He is a deceiver and counterfeiter. In the material world, experts have found that the best way to identify a counterfeit is to become intimately familiar with the real thing. That is vitally true for Christians as we face the master counterfeiter. James 4:7 gives us an unerring strategy for spiritual warfare: "Submit therefore to God. Resist the devil and he will flee from you."

The battlefield in spiritual warfare is primarily the mind. Christian psychologist Archibald Hart states that "the mind defines who we are and creates our environment. Our mind, not our feelings or actions, ultimately shapes our destiny because it is the bridle that holds the power of control." If the mind is the battlefield, then prayer is the believer's weapon of choice.

How we think is fundamental, because the thoughts we have yield consequences. Romans 12:2 counsels us, "Do not be conformed to this world, but be transformed by the renewing of your mind, that you may prove what the will of God is, that which is good and acceptable and perfect." Hart provides insight into how the mind works: "Your whole being is shaped by what resides in your head. Godly character comes from continual right thinking. Keep your thoughts real. Fantasy often leads to disaster."

We live in a world where the devil and his demons seek to control people by influencing their thought life. Discipline is a proven way to break bad habits, even those habits evil has birthed in our lives. God's people must stay attentive and focused. In Matthew 6:33, Jesus said, "Seek first His kingdom and His righteousness." That alone is enough to occupy a lifetime.

Conclusion

The temptation has always existed to make too much of angels and end up worshiping them. It is also possible to disregard the reality of angels and even deny their existence. Because these magnificent spirit beings are so unique to the world we live in, it is possible to make critical mistakes regarding God's angels.

What most Bible teachers and scholars regard as the Colossian heresy involved a convoluted mixture of pagan and Jewish practices and beliefs. It has been referred to as an expression of first-century Jewish legalism mixed with a form of Gnosticism that appeared in the second century. People involved in this heresy claimed to have special insights and esoteric knowledge. When this attitude combined with their confessed mystical experience, the result was not only confusion but heresy.

Paul exposed these self-appointed teachers and pointed out their doctrine of false humility and practice of angel worship. He called their philosophy "empty." The worship of angels is nowhere taught in the Bible. Colossians 2:18-19 says, "Let no one keep defrauding you of your prize by delighting in self-abasement and the worship of the angels, taking his stand on visions he has seen, inflated without cause by his fleshly mind, and not holding fast to the head, from whom the entire body, being supplied and held together by the joints and ligaments, grows with a growth which is from God."

Angels know that only God is the right, or proper, subject of worship. When God revealed to John the Book of Revelation, the apostle experienced powerful and amazing scenes, such as God enthroned in Revelation 21. His experiences were so overwhelming, he was nearly overcome by the sheer magnitude of it all. In Revelation 22:8-9, he wrote, "And I, John, am the one who heard and saw these things. And when I heard and saw, I fell down to worship at the feet of the angel who showed me these things. And he said to me, 'Do not do that; I am a fellow servant of yours and of your brethren the prophets and of those who heed the words of this book; worship God.'"

Angels are wonderful, powerful, incredible, majestic, super intelligent. However, they do not desire our worship and will not accept it. What they do — and what we should do — is to worship the one true God and serve Him obediently.

Thank God for His magnificent angels. As unimaginable as it seems, they serve us. We should honor and respect them by glorifying the God who sent them on their mission of service to us. Always remember that we live in the shadow of the angels.

Resources That Have Influenced the Author

Joan Wester Anderson. *Guardian Angels: True Stories of Answered Prayers*. Loyola Press. Chicago, Illinois. 2006.

Donald Grey Barnhouse. *The Invisible War*. Zondervan Publishing House. Grand Rapids, Michigan. 1965.

Craig L. Blomberg. *The New American Commentary (Volume 22, Matthew)*. Broadman Press. Nashville, Tennessee. 1992.

James Montgomery Boice. *Psalms: An Expositional Commentary (3 volumes)*. Baker Book House. Grand Rapids, Michigan. 1998.

James Petigru Boyce. *Abstract of Systematic Theology*. Copyright 1887. Reprinted by Christian Gospel Foundation.

F.F. Bruce. *The New International Commentary on the New Testament — The Book of Acts*. William B. Eerdmans Publishing Co. Grand Rapids, Michigan. Reprinted February 1983.

John Calvin. *The Institutes of the Christian Religion.* Christian Classics Ethereal Library. Grand Rapids, Michigan. Public Domain.

Jack Canfield, Mark Victor Hansen, Amy Newmark. *Angels Among Us.* Chicken Soup for the Soul Publishing, LLC. 2013.

Richard W. DeHann. *Our Angel Friends: Their Creation, Nature, Distinction, Ministry.* Radio Bible Class. Grand Rapids, Michigan. 1980.

Walter A. Elwell, editor. *Bakers Evangelical Dictionary of Biblical Theology.* Baker Books. Grand Rapids, Michigan. 1996.

Millard J. Erickson. *Christian Theology.* Baker Book House. Grand Rapids, Michigan. Copyright 1983, 1984, 1985.

Tony Evans. *The Truth About Angels.* Moody Publishers. Chicago, Illinois. 2012.

Sinclair B. Ferguson, David F. Wright, J.I. Packer. *New Dictionary of Theology: A Concise and Authoritative Resource.* Intervarsity Press. Downers Grove, Illinois. Leicester, England. 1988.

Billy Graham. *Angels: God's Secret Agents.* Doubleday Publishing Co. Garden City, New York. 1975.

Wayne Grudem. *Systematic Theology.* Zondervan. Grand Rapids, Michigan. 1974.

R. Laird Harris, Gleason L. Archer Jr., Bruce K. Waltke. *Theological Wordbook of the Old Testament. 2 volumes.* Moody Press. Chicago, Illinois. 1980.

Archibald Hart. *Habits of the Mind.* Word Publishing. Dallas, London, Vancouver, Melbourne. 1996.

Michael S. Heiser. *Angels.* Lexham Press. Bellingham, Washington. 2018.

William Hendriksen. *The New Testament Commentary: Exposition of the Gospel According to Matthew.* Baker Book House. Grand Rapids, Michigan. 1975.

Charles Hodge. *Systematic Theology (Vol. 1).* William B. Eerdmans Publishing Company. Grand Rapids, Michigan. Reprinted 1975.

David Jeremiah. *Angels: The Strange and Mysterious Truth.* Multnomah Publishing Inc. Sisters, Oregon. 1996.

C.F. Keil and F. Delitzsch. *Commentary on the Old Testament (Vol. 5, Psalms)*. William B. Eerdmans Publishing Company. Grand Rapids, Michigan. Copyright 1867. Reprinted 1975.

Derek Kidner. *Tyndale Old Testament Commentaries. Psalms 73-150*. Intervarsity Press. London, England. 1975.

Landrum P. Leavell. *Angels, Angels, Angels*. Journey Publications. Metairie, Louisiana. 1973.

John MacArthur Jr. *The MacArthur New Testament Commentary. Matthew*. Moody Bible Institute. Chicago, Illinois. 1985.

John MacArthur Jr. *The MacArthur New Testament Commentary. Acts*. Moody Press. Chicago, Illinois. 1996.

John MacArthur Jr. *The MacArthur New Testament Commentary. Luke (2 vols.)*. Moody Publishers. Chicago, Illinois. 2011.

Judith MacNutt. *Angels Are For Real*. Chosen, a division of Baker Publishing Group. Minneapolis, Minnesota. 2012.

I. Howard Marshall. *New International Greek Testament Commentary. The Gospel of Luke: A Commentary on the Greek Text.* William B. Eerdmans Publishing Company. Grand Rapids, Michigan. 1978.

J. Vernon McGee. *Thru The Bible (5 volumes).* Thomas Nelson Publishers. Nashville, Tennessee. 1983.

John. I. Miller. *Lifted By Angels.* Thomas Nelson Publishers. Nashville, Tennessee. 2012.

James Orr, general editor. *The International Standard Bible Encyclopedia. Volume 1.* Associated Publishers and Authors. Wilmington, Delaware. 1915.

Fritz Rienecker. *A Linguistic Key to the Greek New Testament (2 volumes).* The Zondervan Corporation. Grand Rapids, Michigan. 1978.

A.T. Robertson. *Word Pictures in the Greek New Testament (volumes 1-3).* Broadman Press. Nashville, Tennessee. 1930.

Charles Haddon Spurgeon. *The Treasury of David (3 volumes).* Zondervan Publishing House. Grand Rapids, Michigan. 1966.

Charles Haddon Spurgeon. *Metropolitan Tabernacle Pulpit (volumes 14, 16, 46, 52)*. Pilgrim Publications. Pasadena, Texas. 1970-1978.

Ray Stedman. *Spiritual Warfare*. Waco Books. Waco, Texas. 1978.

Robert H. Stein. *The New American Commentary (vol. 24, Luke)*. Broadman Press. Nashville, Tennessee. 1992.

Augustus H. Strong. *Systematic Theology*. Fleming H. Revell Company. Old Tappan, New Jersey. 1907.

Merrill F. Unger. *Biblical Demonology*. Scripture Press Publications. Wheaton, Illinois. 1952.

Merrill F. Unger. *Ungers Bible Dictionary*. Moody Press. Chicago, Illinois. 1966.

John Woolmer. *Angels*. Monarch Books. Mill Hill, London, and Grand Rapids, Michigan. 2003.

www.ingramcontent.com/pod-product-compliance
Lightning Source LLC
Chambersburg PA
CBHW061500040426
42450CB00008B/1430